FOUNTAS & PINNELL

Genre Prompting Guide
for Fiction

SECTION I

Introduction

Literature genres have been developed through centuries of oral storytelling and written language because writers needed ways to make their meaning clear. When you look at aspects of genre, you see the writers' decisions—the essence of their craft. Everything else—the type of language used, the word choice, the use of dialogue, the structure or organization of the text, and all other writers' decisions—rest on the choice of genre. As readers, your students will find that thinking, talking, and writing about a specific genre will help them better understand the text and expand their own thinking.

Organization of Prompts

In this guide, we have organized fiction prompts by genre, and also by literary elements and text structure. You will notice that the organizational categories change somewhat depending upon the genre. Below is a comprehensive list and descriptions of the categories you will see on these pages.

FICTION GENRES

REALISTIC FICTION An imagined story set in the real world that portrays life as it could be lived today, and focuses on the problems and issues of today.

HISTORICAL FICTION An imagined story set in the real world that portrays life as it might have been lived in the past, and focuses on problems and issues of life in the past.

TRADITIONAL LITERATURE Traditional literature is comprised of stories, written or oral, that have been handed down through the years. These tales often served as entertainment and as an oral record of the history and customs of a people.

MODERN FANTASY Unlike traditional literature, modern fantasy does not come from an oral tradition. But like traditional literature, modern fantasy stories [...] events, places, and people that could not exist in the real w[...] texts can be divided into four more specific genres: a[...] fantasy, and science fiction.

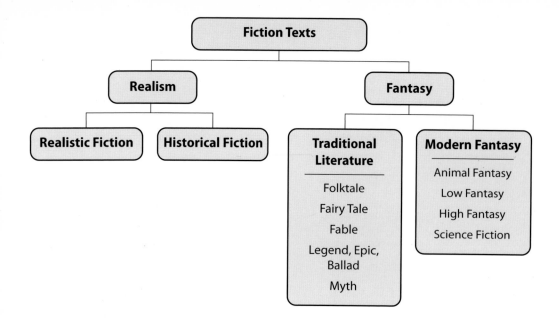

LITERARY ELEMENTS OF FICTION

CHARACTERS are the people, animals, or objects that appear in the story. Readers learn about characters through the writer's descriptions, what the characters think or say, what the characters do, and what others think or say about them.

PLOT refers to the problem of the story, and the events or actions that flow from it.

SETTING is the time and place in which the action happens. Sometimes the setting is relatively unimportant, while at other times, the setting is all-important to the theme and plot.

THEME is the big idea of the story, the author's attitude toward a significant human concern or issue. A writer may weave several themes into one narrative.

PERSPECTIVE refers to the narrator's point of view. The perspective guides the reader.

ELEMENTS OF CRAFT

STYLE AND LANGUAGE Style refers to how the author uses language to convey meaning. Style is not what is said but how it is said. Writers may use figurative language (including simile, metaphor, and personification), imagery, and symbolism to better communicate meaning.

ILLUSTRATIONS/ART meaning is also communicated by the illustrations in a text. Art or photography may extend the meaning far beyond the words. Illustrations also help set the mood and communicate the theme.

DESIGN Closely related to the illustrations is the entire visual presentation of the book—the design. It may contain elements such as size and shape; type of print, font, and layout; integration of illustrations and text; quality of paper and binding; cover design; and end papers.

BELIEVABILITY If anything in a fictional text suddenly reminds you that the story or characters are not real, the story loses credibility and the power to move you.

QUALITY The quality of a text is related to the ways in which the elements work together. A compelling plot, well-developed characters, effective style and language, good use of illustrations, and believability are all related to the quality of a book.

Using *Genre Prompting Guide for Fiction*

The prompts in this guide can be used in any instructional reading context that involves your students in thinking, talking, and writing about reading. Some of the questions will be useful for assigned writing to a prompt or short writes before or after reading (see *Teaching for Comprehending and Fluency: Thinking, Talking, and Writing about Reading, K–8*, Fountas and Pinnell, 2006).

*Note this important caution: the prompts are meant to provide you with lines of inquiry or aspects of texts worthy of discussion. They are not designed for you to pose question after question to your students. You may use some as statements to show readers new ways to think about a text, and later invite them to apply that thinking to a new text. Or you may tell your students that you noticed that they were thinking about an important aspect of text. Many of the prompts are expressed with academic language and fairly sophisticated vocabulary. You can teach your students this language over time. Rephrase the prompts if students do not understand the prompts at first.

INTERACTIVE READ-ALOUD: In this whole group context, you and your students think together about a text you read aloud. Stop in a few places to invite thinking or to have students turn and talk about their thinking to a partner or in threes.

SHARED READING: Usually refers to students reading from a common enlarged text, either a large-print book, a chart, or a projected text. Students may have their own copies. The teacher leads the group, pointing to words or phrases. Reading is usually in unison, although there are adaptations, such as groups alternating lines or individuals reading some lines.

BOOK CLUBS OR LITERATURE DISCUSSION GROUPS: In a small group book discussion, invite students' thinking so they can build a richer meaning than any one reader could construct from the text.

GUIDED READING; INTRODUCTION TO THE TEXT, DISCUSSION OF THE TEXT, REVISITING THE TEXT: In this small group context, use prompts to get students thinking in the introduction to the text and build a deeper meaning in the discussion after reading the text. You may choose to revisit a page, paragraph, or sentence for close reading. Close reading involves thinking together about the text to explore interpretations of the author's meaning.

READING CONFERENCES: In individual conferences with readers, you can use these prompts to prompt students to share their thinking about books they are reading independently.

WRITING ABOUT READING (responses in readers' notebooks, test writing): When you read your students' writing about reading, refer to the prompts to use in conferring or extending thinking in your written response.

General Prompts to Support Comprehension of Fiction

FICTION is invented, imaginative prose or poetry. Fiction texts are usually narrative and can be organized into the categories of realism and fantasy. Along with nonfiction, fiction is one of two basic genres of literature.

Characteristics of the Genre

What is the genre?

What characteristics help you to figure out the genre?

Why is this text a good example of the genre?

How is this book like other books you've read in this genre?

What are some of the challenges of reading books in this genre?

What kind of story is the author telling?

How do you know this story is fiction?

How do you know this is science fiction (or other fiction) genre?

Could the story really happen?

Characters

Who are the important characters (people/animals) in the story?

Who are some of the other characters that are not important? Why do you think the author included them?

What character does the writer tell mostly about?

How would you describe a character you like or care most about? Why do you like that character?

Who are the powerful characters and what makes them powerful (weak)?

What are the character traits of the most interesting character in the story?

How would you describe the main character?

How would you describe the fairest (kindest, most helpful/generous) character?

How would you describe the bravest (most daring) character?

Characters *(continued)*

What lesson did the characters teach you?

What characters would you add to the story? Why?

What choices did the character (name) have?

How does the author/illustrator reveal the character? (Look at what the character does, thinks, or says; or what others say about the character.)

How and why does the character change?

How is character change important to the story?

How would you describe one of the minor characters from the story? Why is this character important to the story?

How do characters feel about each other?

What decisions do the characters have to make?

How do these decisions affect other people in the story?

How does the author make the characters believable?

How do the characters' actions contribute to the sequence of events?

How would you compare the two characters (names) from the story?

Plot

How does the author engage the reader right from the beginning?

What is the problem in the story?

What is one action that the characters take to solve the problem?

How do your predict the problem will be resolved?

What helps the characters solve the problem?

What are the challenges that the characters face and how do they deal with them?

What was the most important part of the story?

How would you describe the story shape? (linear, triangular, circular: for example, home-adventure-home)

Plot *(continued)*

What are the important events in the story?

What is the high point of the story?

What is the order of events in the story? (for example, series of sequential events, letter or diary, record, flashback)

How could the order of events be changed? Could some be left out? Why?

How did the story end? Were your predictions correct?

How would you have ended the story? Why?

What clues does the author give that allow you to predict the ending?

What lesson(s) does this story teach about life?

What do you think will happen next in the story? After the story ends?

What do you think will happen next for the characters after the story ends?

What information or details does the author give to make the story seem realistic or believable?

How does the author show the time or how the time has changed?

What techniques does the author use to make you feel that you are really there? (in both realistic stories and fantasy)

How was the problem resolved?

How would you summarize the story in two or three sentences?

What are some questions that are still unanswered?

What type of conflict is depicted in this story? (person against (1) person, (2) self, (3) society, (4) nature).

What is an example of foreshadowing, flashback, rising action, climax, or falling action from the story?

What is an example of suspense from the text?

Where in the story do you see an example of a cliffhanger?

Setting

Where and when does the story take place?

Where else could the story take place?

Is it possible that the setting could be a real place that exists in our time? Why do you think so?

How is the setting important to the story?

What words did the author use to describe the place?

What can you hear, see, feel or, smell as you read?

How important is the place or time to the story?

How much time passes in the story?

In another time or place, how would the story change?

How does the author show the passing of time?

How is the setting similar to a place you know?

How does the season or the time affect the characters or plot of the story?

Is the setting integral to the plot or just a backdrop?

Is the setting a source of conflict or the adversary? (e.g., people against nature)

How does the setting contribute to the mood or tone of the story?

Is the setting symbolic (does it represent good, evil, home, alienation)?

How would you compare this setting to others in stories written by the same author?

How would you compare different settings from the story?

Theme

What is (are) the author's message(s)?

What is the story really about?

Why is the title appropriate for the story?

What does the story mean to you?

Theme *(continued)*

Why did the author write the story?

What is the author really trying to say?

How does the writer communicate the theme (explicitly, implicitly)?

What are the secondary themes?

What central truth about the human condition is the author trying to communicate?

What moral or inspirational lesson is the author trying to teach?

What comment about human nature or society is the author attempting to communicate?

What key details support the message, moral, or lesson from a fable, folktale, or myth?

How would you compare the themes of stories by the same author in books that have similar or the same characters?

How would you compare similar themes in the story, myth or other traditional literature?

Perspective

Why did the author choose the main character to tell the story?

Why is this character the best person to tell the story, or the best person to use as the main character?

Whose point of view is used in the story?

What other voices could tell the story?

How would the story be different if told through another person's voice?

How do you know who is telling the story?

Where do you see an example of the narrator talking directly to the reader?

How has the author created a narrator with an objective point of view?

Perspective *(continued)*

What kind of narrator has the author chosen to tell the story?

- anonymous outsider who reveals everything about the main and supporting characters through actions, dialogue, and thoughts (third person, *he, she, they*)

- anonymous outsider who mainly reveals the main character's point of view through actions, dialogue, and thoughts (third person, *he, she, they*)

Why do you think the author chose a narrator with an objective point of view that offers only description and leaves interpretation to the reader?

How does the narrator's perspective influence how the events are described?

Style and Language

What are some interesting words, phrases, or sentences the author uses?

What are some words that were used to create a feeling or picture in your mind?

What is an example of a well-written description in this book?

What are examples of language that you found especially interesting, vivid, or surprising?

What are some of the strongest words the author uses?

How does the author begin/end the story?

What words or phrases are memorable or special?

What are some examples of poetic language?

What are some examples of playful, whimsical, or connotative language that the writer uses?

Figurative Language

What words did the writer use to describe/compare the character?

What did the author say the person or object is like?

What did the writer compare the (character, object, action) to?

What was the writer trying to say about the person?

What are some examples of figurative language that the writer uses?

Figurative Language *(continued)*

Can you find an example of language used to compare things (metaphor, simile)?

Why did the writer personify _____? What words did the writer use?

Imagery

What images did the writing evoke?

How did the author use language to evoke images?

What words, phrases, or sentences does the author use to make you see (hear, feel, smell, taste) what it was like?

Symbolism

What are some examples of symbolism?

Are the setting or events symbolic in any way?

What symbols can you find that are typical for the genre?

Mood/Tone

How does the story make you feel?

What makes you feel that way?

Does the mood or tone change?

Describe a point in the story where your feelings changed.

What are some examples of serious, humorous, or absurd moments or events that you noticed in the text?

How do descriptions of the setting or people's actions contribute to the mood of the text?

What words would you use to describe the mood of the story?

How does dialogue contribute to the mood of the story?

How does your own connection to the story contribute to the mood?

How does your own connection to the story help you feel the mood?

Illustrations/Art

How do the illustrations add to the story?

How important are the illustrations?

What is the role of illustrations in conveying the meaning of the story?

What is your favorite illustration? Why?

Could you picture what was happening when there was no illustration?

What can you learn about the setting from the illustrations?

How do the illustrations contribute to the mood or tone of the story?

How are the illustrations related to the point of view?

What do the illustrations reveal about the characters?

Are the illustrations important/critical to your understanding of the story?

Did the style of the illustrations match the tone of the story?

Author/Illustrator

Would you read other books by this author? Why?

Would you read other books by this illustrator? Why?

If you have read other books by this author, what are the similarities and differences between the books?

If you have read other books by this illustrator, what are the similarities and differences between the books?

What other books does this book make you want to read?

Why do you think this particular author wrote this book?

What background knowledge did the author need in order to write this book?

What did the author do to interest the reader or pull the reader into the text?

How did the author keep you interested in the book?

Why do you think the author began/ended the story this way?

How does this author's style compare to that of other authors who have written about the same theme or in the same genre?

Author/Illustrator *(continued)*

Why did the author choose this title? Was it a good choice?

What title would you have chosen?

What do you notice about the style of the author's writing?

What information did the author provide in a foreword, introduction, or afterword?

Design

What did you notice about the design of the book?

Does the book have special features, such as border designs?

How does the design of the book influence your opinion of the book as a whole?

Does the design of the book reflect the genre?

How does the design of the book compare to the design of other (genre-specific) books you have read?

Believability

Do the characters behave in a way that is expected for the genre?

Do the events and artifacts in the story fit the genre?

Does the dialogue between characters seem authentic to the genre?

Are the characters' emotions and actions presented in a way that is believable given what you know about them?

Quality

Is the plot compelling?

Are the characters well developed?

Is the author's writing style and use of language effective?

Do the illustrations support and enhance the story?

Is the story believable?

Do all of the elements work together?

Realistic Fiction

REALISTIC FICTION is an imagined story set in the real world that portrays life as it could be lived today, and focuses on the problems and issues of today.

Characteristics of the Genre

What is the genre? How do you know?

What kind of realistic fiction is this book (humor, animal story, sports, school, or mystery)?

How is this book like other books in this genre?

What characteristics in the story made you classify it as realistic fiction?

Is this story a good (or poor) example of realistic fiction?

How does this story compare to another realistic fiction novel on the same topic or theme?

How does the structure of the text help to convey the meaning of the story?

How is this story different from a historical fiction text?

How is this story different from a nonfiction text?

How is this story different from a fantasy or science fiction text?

What are some of the challenges of reading books in this genre?

Characters

Who are the characters? Are they portrayed accurately in light of your knowledge of cultures and issues?

How does the author reveal the characters?

How has the author made these characters seem real?

How does the author portray the characters (good, evil, a combination)?

Do any of the characters change? Is that change consistent with your knowledge of the issues or events in the book? Is the change believable?

What connections do you share with any of the characters?

Characters *(continued)*

Which characters remind you of someone in your life?

How do you feel about the choices that the characters made?

What motivates the characters' actions and decisions?

What choices would you have made if you were the character?

Do you agree or disagree with the character's choices?

Which characters were portrayed in a stereotypical way according to their race, gender, culture, age, religion, physical or mental differences?

How are people of color portrayed?

How is the culture of the character(s) similar to or different from your culture?

Did any of the characters change from the beginning to the end of the story?

Plot

How do the events and circumstances in the book compare to current ones?

How is the problem in the story tied to the events in the story?

What events in the story connect to events in your own life?

How does your knowledge of the issue(s) or problem help you to predict how the events will unfold?

What challenges do the characters face that are different from ones that you have faced?

How is the ending authentic?

What are some of the significant events that shape the plot?

What are some specific details that describe an important event in the story?

What alternative events and endings can you think of?

How do you think the story will end based on the characters' attributes and actions?

Based on your own experience and/or knowledge of current issues, what do you think will happen to the characters after the story ends?

Setting

What is the setting? Is it described accurately?

How does the time period have an effect on the plot?

How much time passes over the course of the story?

How is the setting important to the story?

How would the story change in a different time or place?

How does the author create a realistic and authentic setting?

Why do you think the author chose this particular setting to tell this story?

How does the setting make the story more authentic?

Could this story take place right now or do elements related to the setting seem outdated?

Theme

What is (are) the author's message(s)?

What is this story really about?

What does the story make you think about?

What are some of the details that help you get to the big ideas in the book?

Is (are) the theme(s) obvious (explicitly stated), or unstated?

What common themes did you notice in the text (survival, courage, death and dying, poverty, upward mobility, persistence, family relationships, tragedy)?

What are some of the recurring themes in other realistic fiction novels you have read?

How does this story compare to a novel or movie about the same issue?

Why do you think the author chose this setting and how is it related to the message?

How do you think the author's message applies to your life?

What new ideas or perspectives about a culture or issue have you gained by reading this text?

What is the author trying to say about current issues?

Theme *(continued)*

How do issues in the story relate to issues that have appeared recently in the media? To current events?

Perspective

From whose perspective is this story told?

Why is this character the best person to tell the story?

What is the author's perspective?

How are the perspectives of other characters in conflict with the narrator's perspective?

What perspectives in the book do you agree or disagree with?

How would the story be different if it were told from a different perspective?

How are perspectives of different cultures accurately represented?

Style and Language

What are some examples of language the author uses to give the story a realistic feel?

How does the author's language style contribute to the story's genre?

How do the words or style of speaking help to determine the setting?

How does the author use dialogue to give the story a realistic feel?

What words or phrases did the author use to make the story sound modern?

How did the author use words from another language to make the story more culturally relevant?

Figurative Language

Does the author use simile or metaphor to communicate meaning?

What are some examples of simile or metaphor that the author uses?

Does the author personify any objects or animals? Why?

Imagery

How does the author use language to appeal to the reader's senses?

How does the language in the story help you to see, smell, feel, or hear what is happening in the story?

Symbolism

What symbols does the author use to convey meaning? Are these symbols you are familiar with, or are they unique to this story?

How does the author's use of symbolism help you to better understand the story? Better understand the author's message(s)?

Mood/Tone

What is the mood or tone of this story?

What language does the author use to help establish the mood of the story?

What other elements help to establish the mood of the story (comparisons, illustrations, other design features)?

In what ways does the mood or tone of the story change?

Illustrations/Art

How do the illustrations help set the mood or tone of the story?

How do the illustrations help convey the theme of the story?

How do the illustrations extend the meaning of the story beyond the words?

What clues do the illustrations give about setting and characters?

Do the illustrations help to make the story feel authentic or real?

What is the illustrator's style?

What media does the illustrator use?

How does the illustrator's style affect your opinion of the story?

How does the illustrator's style contribute to the contemporary feel of the book?

What connections do the illustrations have to your own life?

Design

What did you notice about the design of the book?

Does the book have special features, such as border designs?

How does the design of the book affect your opinion of the book as a whole?

Is the design of the book related to the topic, theme, or setting of the book? How?

Believability

Do the characters behave in a realistic way for people of their age group and culture?

Do the events and artifacts in the story fit the time period and setting?

Does the dialogue between characters seem real?

Does the story end in a way that seems plausible?

Are the characters' emotions and actions presented in a way that is believable?

Do the characters in the story behave like real people would in a similar situation?

How believable is the book compared to another book you have read on the same topic or theme?

How do details about food, cooking, clothing, and transportation contribute to the believability of the text?

Does the author use current issues to make the story more believable?

Were there any implausible coincidences in the story? Why were they unbelievable?

Do you think the author left anything out that would have made the story more believable?

Quality

Is the plot compelling?

Are the characters well developed?

Is the author's writing style and use of language effective?

Do the illustrations support and enhance the story?

Is the story believable?

Do all of the elements work together?

Historical Fiction

HISTORICAL FICTION is an imagined story set in the real world that portrays life as it might have been lived in the past, and focuses on problems and issues of life in the past.

Characteristics of the Genre

What is the genre? How do you know?

How is this book like other books in this genre?

What characteristics in the story help you classify it as historical fiction?

Is this story a good (or poor) example of historical fiction?

How does this story compare to another historical fiction novel that you have read on the same topic or theme?

How is this historical fiction story different from an informational text about the same period?

How is this historical fiction story different from or similar to realistic fiction?

What new understandings and historical information do you have after reading this story?

What are the challenges of reading historical fiction?

What aspect of the book has been fictionalized (characters, plot, setting, events)?

Characters

Who are the characters? Are they portrayed accurately for the time period in which the story takes place?

Are any of the characters based on real people?

Do the characters that the author has invented seem as believable as those based on real people?

How has the author made the characters seem real to readers of today?

What problem drives or motivates the main character?

Are the pressures on the main character related to the time period or setting?

What can you learn from the characters' actions?

Characters *(continued)*

What critical choices did the characters have to make? Were these choices heroic (difficult, consistent with character traits)?

How did each character react to the important events of the story?

How are the main character's choices influenced by society or culture?

How are the character's choices influenced by the historical time period or the setting?

What challenges did people who lived during this time period face?

What are the main character's motivations and how are they related to the historical setting?

Do any of the characters change? How is that change consistent with your knowledge of the time period?

Are people of color portrayed in a way that is consistent with your knowledge of the time period?

What connections do you share with any of the characters?

How are the challenges that the characters face different from the ones that you face today?

Even though the story takes place in a different time, have you had similar experiences as any of the characters?

How did these historical characters remind you of people that you know?

Plot

Which events has the author made up and which really happened?

Do the events described in the story seem authentic and real?

How does the time period influence the plot?

What details does the author use to bring the historic events to life?

How does your knowledge of the time period help you to predict how the events in the story will unfold?

What changes take place in the story? How are those changes significant?

Plot *(continued)*

What is the sequence of events in the story? Is this sequence historically accurate?

What are some of the historical details that shape the plot?

What event from the story was especially significant to you?

How are the events in the story related to the historical setting?

How is the problem in the story tied to historical events?

What significant historical events were taking place at the time of the story?

How is your understanding of the problem influenced by your understanding of the historical time or events?

Which events could not happen today?

What problems in the story are still relevant today?

Are any of the historical events in this story similar to current ones?

How is the ending authentic to the time period?

What events in the story connect to events in your own life?

What new information about this period in history have you learned?

Setting

What is the setting?

What is the time period?

What kind of place is this? What does it feel like?

What do you know about the time period?

What details do you notice about the setting and what it feels like?

Were there jumps in time in the story?

What is changing in the historical times of the story?

How does the author establish or convey the setting and time period?

How does the description of the place help you to determine when in history this story is set?

At what point in the story were you able to determine the historical setting?

Setting *(continued)*

What clues helped you to determine the historical setting?

Why do you think the author chose this particular time in history and the setting to tell this story?

How are the time period and setting important to the story?

How would the story be different if it were set in a different time or place?

What details does the author use to create an historically accurate setting?

What did you learn about the time period from this story?

What is a timeline of the historical content in this story?

What do you want to learn more about the time period after reading this story?

Theme

What is (are) the author's message(s)?

What is this story really about?

What does the story make you think about?

What are some of the details that help you get to the big ideas in the book?

What do you think the author was trying to say about this time period?

What message(s) does the author want to convey in this story and how does (do) it (they) relate to the time period?

How does the time period help to convey the particular theme of the story?

Is (are) the message(s) of the story still relevant today?

How do you think the author's messages apply to today's world?

Which recurring theme of historical fiction did you notice in the book (clash of cultures, search for freedom, overcoming physical challenges, effects of war, effects of natural disasters, struggle against evil or tyranny or other)?

What are some recurring themes in other historical fiction stories you have read?

What big ideas does this book share with other books you have read?

What new ideas or perspectives have you gained by reading this book?

How can the lessons of this story be applied to life today?

Perspective

From whose perspective is this story told?

Why did the author choose this character to tell the story?

What is the author's perspective?

How are the perspectives of other characters in conflict with the narrator's perspective?

What perspectives in the book do you agree or disagree with?

How would the story be different if it were told from a different perspective?

How is this perspective influenced by the historical context?

How are the perspectives of the main or minor characters influenced by the historical context?

How does the author show his/her own interest and/or attitude towards the historical times?

Style and Language

How does the author's style contribute to the story's genre?

How do the words or style of speaking help to determine the setting or time period?

How does the author use dialogue to give the story a historical feel?

What are some examples of the language the author uses to give the story a historical feel?

What are some examples of language that is authentic to the time period?

How does the author use words to reveal the characters?

How does the author use dialogue to make the characters and setting more authentic to the time period?

How is the author's style similar to that in other books written about the same time period?

Figurative Language

Does the author use simile or metaphor to communicate meaning?

What are some examples of simile or metaphor that the author uses?

How has the author used figurative language to help you understand the historical setting?

Imagery

How does the author use imagery that is specific to the time period?

How does the language in the story help you to immerse yourself in the time period?

Symbolism

What symbols does the author use to convey meaning? Are the symbols specific to the time period?

How does the author use symbolism to help you to better understand the story?

Mood/Tone

What is the mood or tone of this story?

What language does the author use to help establish the mood of the story?

What other elements help to establish the mood of the story?

In what ways does the mood or tone of the story change?

Illustrations/Art

How does the illustrator help the reader to understand the historical time in which the story is set?

What clues to the setting or meaning do you get through illustrations or other features?

What historical information is provided through the illustrations?

How important are the illustrations to your understanding of the historical period?

Illustrations/Art *(continued)*

How important are the illustrations to your understanding of the genre?

What do the illustrations add to the story?

How do the illustrations contribute to the mood or tone of the story?

How does the illustrator's style support the mood and setting of the story?

How does the illustrator's style influence your opinion of the book?

What medium does the illustrator use? Why is that a good choice for this book?

What is a specific illustration that helped you to understand the time period?

Design

What did you notice about the design of the book?

Does the book have special features, such as border designs? How do they add to the story?

How does the design of the book affect your opinion of the book as a whole?

Does the design of the book reflect the genre? In what ways?

Believability

Do the characters behave in a realistic way for people of the time period?

Do the characters in the story behave like real people would in a similar situation?

Do the events and artifacts in the story fit the time period and setting?

Does the dialogue between characters seem authentic to the time period and setting?

Does the story end in a way that seems plausible?

Are the characters' emotions and actions presented in a way that is believable?

How believable is the book compared to another historical fiction book you have read set in the same time period?

How do historical details about food, cooking, clothing, and transportation contribute to the believability of the text?

Believability *(continued)*

Does the author use issues that were important during that time period to make the story more believable?

Do you think the author left anything out that would have made the story more believable?

Quality

Is the plot compelling?

Are the characters well developed?

Is the author's writing style and use of language effective?

Do the illustrations support and enhance the story?

Is the story believable?

Do all of the elements work together?

Traditional Literature

TRADITIONAL LITERATURE is comprised of stories, written or oral, that have been handed down through the years. These tales often served as entertainment and as an oral record of the history and customs of a people.

Characteristics of the Genre

What is the genre? How do you know?

What kind of traditional tale is this story (cumulative, pourquoi, beast, noodlehead or numbskull, trickster, realistic, fairy tale, tall tale, myth, legend, epic)?

How is this book like other books in this genre?

What characteristics in the story help you classify it as traditional literature?

Is this story a good (or poor) example of traditional literature?

How does this book compare to another book of the same genre, with the same theme?

How does this story compare to other types of fiction?

How does this story compare to a modern work of fiction that draws on the same themes, patterns of events, or types of characters?

What are some of the challenges of reading traditional literature?

Characters

Who are the characters? Are they portrayed realistically even though they may not be real?

Do characters seem human even though they may not be possible characters in the real world?

What kinds of characters are typically found in traditional stories?

How does the author reveal the characters?

How does the author portray the characters (good, evil, a combination)?

How does the culture of the story influence the portrayal of the characters?

Do the characters make good (bad) choices?

Characters *(continued)*

What influences the characters' choices?

What motivates the characters' actions and decisions?

What choices would you have made if you were the character?

Why do you agree or disagree with a character's choices?

What connections do you share with any of the characters?

What challenges do the characters face that are different to the ones that you face?

Are there any flat or stereotypical characters (good, bad, tricky, lazy, hardworking, timid, brave, etc.)?

What kinds of traditional characters does the author use (talking animals, magical creatures or people, royalty, etc.)?

How does this make the story more interesting?

How does the author make the characters seem believable?

How would you use the magic in the story differently from a character in the story?

Who was your favorite character? What made that character likeable?

Who is the hero in the story and what attributes does he/she possess?

Why do you think the author chose to use animals as the main characters?

What magical powers did characters have? Would you choose to have those powers?

Plot

What were the important events from the story?

How is the problem in the story tied to the events?

How does your knowledge of traditional stories help you to predict how the events in this story will unfold?

What is an event from the story that you can't forget?

Plot *(continued)*

What quest are the characters on?

What events in the story connect to events in your own life?

How does the structure of the text help to convey meaning or support the genre?

What are some alternative events or endings that would make sense in this story?

How do you think the story will end based on the characters' attributes and decisions?

What information and details does the author provide to make the story seem realistic even though it couldn't happen?

Based on your own experience and/or knowledge of traditional literature, what do you predict will happen to the characters after the book ends?

Could the problem in this story have been resolved without the use of magic? How?

How is the problem often resolved in traditional literature?

Setting

Where does the story take place?

How is the setting important to the story?

How is the setting like a real place?

What parts of the setting seem real and what parts seem like fantasy?

How would the story be different in a different time or place?

How does the setting make the story more magical?

How does the author create a magical place?

Do the characters behave in ways that are true to the setting?

Do the events of the story unfold in a way that is true to the setting?

Why do you think the author chose this particular setting to tell the story?

Does the setting help to convey the message of the story?

How does this setting compare to settings in other traditional literature stories?

Theme

What is this story really about?

What does the story make you think about?

What are some of the details that help you get to the big ideas in the story?

What is (are) the author's message(s)?

Why do you think the author chose this genre and how does it support his/her message?

What are some of the recurring themes in the traditional stories you have read?

What are some of the common motifs/patterns found in traditional literature (magical powers, transformations, magic objects, wishes, trickery, clever young or small person, patterns)?

How do the events and characters in this story compare to those in realistic and historical fiction stories you have read?

How does this story compare to similar stories or movies from other cultures?

What is the author trying to say about society?

What common themes did you find in the text (good vs. evil, good triumphing over evil, greed, etc.)?

What new ideas or perspectives about a culture have you gained by reading this text?

How can the lesson or moral of the story be applied to your own life?

How are the issues in the story similar to issues that people have today?

How is this story similar to and different from other tales that have similar motifs (quests, villains, tricksters)?

How would you summarize the story, including the message, lesson, or moral and how it is conveyed?

Perspective

From whose perspective is this story told?

Why did the author choose this character to tell the story?

What is the author's perspective?

How are the perspectives of other characters in conflict with the narrator's perspective? Or with the perspective of the main character?

What perspectives in the book do you agree or disagree with?

How would the story be different if it were told from a different perspective?

How are perspectives of different cultures accurately represented?

Style and Language

What are some examples of language the author uses to reflect the traditional tale (the culture from which the tale comes)?

How does the author's style support the genre?

How does the language help to establish the setting and make it seem authentic?

How does the author use dialogue to give the story a traditional feel?

What are some words or phrases from the story that are typically found in traditional stories?

Why does the author use words or expressions from another language?

What repetitions or patterns of language do you find in the story?

What language did the author use to show that the story took place a long time ago?

Figurative Language

Does the author use simile or metaphor to communicate meaning?

What are some examples of simile or metaphor that the author uses?

How has the author used figurative language to help you understand the genre?

Imagery

What imagery does the author use that is typically found in traditional stories?

How does the language in the story help you to immerse yourself in the setting?

Symbolism

What symbols does the author use to convey meaning? Are the symbols specific to (commonly used in) traditional literature?

How does the author's use of symbolism help you to better understand the story?

Mood/Tone

What is the mood or tone of this story?

What language does the author use to help establish the mood of the story?

What other elements help to establish the mood of the story?

In what ways does the mood or tone of the story change?

Illustrations and Art

What clues to the setting or meaning do you get through illustrations or other features?

What items does the illustrator include in the drawings to make the story seem magical or old-fashioned?

How does the illustrator use illustrations to make the characters come alive?

How does the illustrator's style contribute to the magical feel of the book?

What connections do the illustrations have to your own life?

Do any of the illustrations promote stereotypes?

Design

What did you notice about the design of the book?

Does the book have special features, such as border designs?

How does the design of the book affect your opinion of the book as a whole?

Does the design of the book reflect the genre?

How does the design of the book compare to the design of realistic fiction books you have read?

Believability

Do the characters behave in a way that is expected for the genre?

Do the events and artifacts in the story fit the genre?

Does the dialogue between characters seem authentic to the genre?

Are the characters' emotions and actions presented in a way that is believable given what you know about them?

How does the author make characters believable even though they could not exist in the real world?

Quality

Is the plot compelling?

Are the characters well developed?

Is the author's writing style and use of language effective?

Do the illustrations support and enhance the story?

Is the story believable?

Do all of the elements work together?

Folktales

FOLKTALE is a form of traditional literature that often features the exploits of ordinary people or "folk." Folktales have a narrative structure, written or oral, and have been handed down over many years.

Characteristics of the Genre

What kind of folktale is this?

What makes this story a beast tale (cumulative tale, pourquoi tale, trickster tale, noodlehead or fool tale, realistic tale, tall tale)?

What makes this story a good (poor) example of a beast tale (cumulative tale, pourquoi tale, trickster tale, noodlehead or fool tale, realistic tale, tall tale)?

Which ideas or descriptions were exaggerated? Is there any way that they could be true and not exaggerations?

In what kind of folktales do you most often see exaggerations?

Characters

How does the author describe the characters?

What more would you like to know about the characters?

Are the characters in the story portrayed as good, evil, or a combination of both?

How difficult is it to determine which characters are good and which are evil?

What common traits do you see in the main characters? How are characters portrayed as strong or clever?

Are the good characters always portrayed as clever or strong?

How are the good characters rewarded?

How are the evil characters punished?

How do you feel when good characters are rewarded and evil characters are punished?

In what ways do the animals act like humans?

How do you know that the tricksters in the story are clever?

What tricks do the characters play on each other?

Characters *(continued)*

How are other characters tricked?

Which characters seem foolish or funny to you?

What impact on the story do silly characters have?

Plot

What natural phenomenon is explained?

Does the explanation seem realistic?

How difficult is the plot to follow or understand?

Do folktales tend to have difficult or simple plot structures? Why do you think that is true?

Why do you think the story is short? Does it need to be longer?

How quickly does the action occur?

Is the ending of the tale predictable?

How are problems resolved?

Setting

What is the setting?

Is the setting important to the story?

Does the setting seem based on a real or an imaginary place?

How does the setting contribute to the plot?

How does the setting help to convey the theme?

Theme

What is (are) the author's message(s)?

What does this tale make you think about?

Is there always justice in folktales?

Can lessons learned in this tale be applied to life today?

Perspective

From whose perspective is this tale told?

What is the author's perspective?

What perspectives in the book do you agree or disagree with?

How would the story be different if it were told from a different perspective?

Style and Language

Which sentences, phrases or chants are repeated in the story?

Why does the author repeat certain sentences, phrases or chants?

Why would this story be easy to recite from memory?

Figurative Language

Does the author use simile or metaphor to communicate meaning?

What are some examples of simile or metaphor that the author uses?

How has the author used figurative language to help you understand the genre?

Imagery

What imagery does the author use that is typically found in folktales?

How does the language in the story help you to immerse yourself in the setting?

Symbolism

What symbols does the author use to convey meaning?

What significance do the numbers 3 and 7 have?

How are numbers used in a symbolic way?

How does the author's use of symbolism help you to better understand the story?

Mood/Tone

What is the mood or tone of this story?

What language does the author use to help establish the mood of the story?

What other elements help to establish the mood of the story?

Fairy Tales

FAIRY TALES (also called "wonder tales") are a type of folktale that emphasizes magic and the supernatural.

Characteristics of the Genre

What type of traditional tale is this?

What parts of the story help you to identify it as a fairy tale?

What other versions of this story have you read?

How is this story different from other versions of the story that you have read?

Characters

What magical powers do the characters have?

How would you use the magical powers that are in the story?

In what ways (good, evil) do the characters use their magical powers?

How do humans and animals interact?

Who are the "good" characters?

Who are the "evil" ("bad") characters?

How does the writer distinguish good characters from "evil" ("bad") characters?

Which characters have a combination of good and evil traits?

Which characters are flawed?

Why would the writer include characters with flaws?

What do the flawed characters add to the story?

What problems do the characters have?

How are the problems realistic or unrealistic?

What connections do you have with the characters' problems?

What problems do the characters have that are similar to problems you or people in your life have?

How were the characters able to complete the tasks they had set for them?

Characters *(continued)*

What character traits helped the character(s) complete the tasks?

What character traits prevented the character(s) from completing the tasks?

What happens to the "good" characters at the end of the story?

What happens to the "bad" characters at the end of the story?

How do the characters change by the end of the story?

Plot

How do the characters use their magical powers to solve the problem in the story?

Could the problems in this story have been solved without the use of magical powers?

How are the events in the story related to the tasks the characters must complete?

Which tasks seem impossible to complete?

How would you describe the tasks (humorous, frightening, life-threatening, etc.)?

How were the characters able to complete the tasks?

What prevented the characters from completing the tasks?

What happens to the "good" characters at the end of the story?

What happens to the "bad" characters at the end of the story?

What punishment do the "bad" characters receive?

Why would you describe the ending of the story as happy (sad)?

Who "lived happily ever after" and who did not?

Setting

Would you describe the setting as medieval?

How is a historic setting important to the plot?

How does the setting impact the events in the story?

Theme

What is (are) the author's message(s)?

What does this story make you think about?

Would you describe the characters as exacting revenge or receiving justice?

What happens to the "bad" characters at the end of the story?

What punishment do the "bad" characters receive? What did they learn?

What message does the writer want you to learn by punishing the bad characters?

What message can you learn when good characters succeed?

Perspective

From whose perspective is this tale told?

What is the author's perspective?

What perspectives in the book do you agree or disagree with?

How would the story be different if it were told from a different perspective?

Style and Language

How does the animal speech remind you of human speech?

What speech patterns do the animals use?

What common language like "once upon a time" or "long ago" did you notice in the story?

How does the writer make it sound like someone is telling a story?

Figurative Language

Does the author use simile or metaphor to communicate meaning?

What are some examples of simile or metaphor that the author uses?

How has the author used figurative language to help you understand the genre?

Imagery

What imagery does the author use that is typically found in fairy tales?

How does the language in the story help you to immerse yourself in the setting?

Symbolism

What symbols does the author use to convey meaning?

How does the author's use of symbolism help you to better understand the story?

Mood/Tone

What is the mood or tone of this story?

What language does the author use to help establish the mood of the story?

What other elements help to establish the mood of the story?

Fables

FABLES are brief, moralistic tales that are primarily meant to instruct.

Characteristics of the Genre

What type of traditional tale is this?

What parts of the story help you to identify it as a fable?

What other versions of this story have you read?

How is this story different from other versions of the story that you have read?

Characters

How are the main characters portrayed (animals, elements of nature)?

How does the writer make the main characters seem human?

How does the number of characters in the story compare to other traditional tales?

Are characters well developed (complex) or flat (one-dimensional)?

What is an example of a character that is flat? What is an example of a character that is well developed?

How do the attributes of the characters (lazy, good, bad, tricky) define them?

Do the characters behave in predictable ways?

Why doesn't the writer give the characters names?

Which human traits do the characters represent?

Plot

How does the title help you know what is going to happen?

Are the events in the story predictable?

How does your knowledge of fables help you to predict the outcome?

How is the plot in this story similar to that in other fables you have read?

Setting

Where does the story take place?

Why is the setting important to the plot and/or message of the story?

How does the setting help the author to convey the message or moral of the story?

Theme

How does the length of the story help to convey the message?

What lesson(s) does the fable teach?

What connection do you have to the lesson?

In what context have you heard this lesson before?

How does the writer deliver the lesson?

Did you know what the lesson was before you read the moral?

How does the lesson match the story?

What universal truths does the fable illustrate?

Legends, Epics, Ballads

LEGENDS, EPICS, and **BALLADS** are long narrative stories that usually revolve around the actions of a single hero. Ballads have a musical quality to them, while epics are told in a more elevated style.

Characteristics of the Genre

What type of traditional literature is this?

What similarities do you notice about this legend (epic, ballad) and other legends (epics, ballads) you have read or heard?

Why does the length of the story matter? Why does it include more than one story?

How would the story be different if it was told in prose rather than poetic verse?

Characters

How does the length of the text impact the plot or characters in the story?

Who is the hero/heroine in the story?

How does the hero/heroine in this story compare to other heroes/heroines that you have read about?

How do heroes/heroines differ by culture or country?

How are American legends or heroes/heroines different or similar to heroes/heroines or legends from other countries?

How are the hero's/heroine's attributes exaggerated?

How are the values of the culture represented in the hero/heroine of the story?

What happens to characters who violate those values?

What weakness(es) must the hero/heroine overcome?

What special attributes does the hero/heroine have?

How does the hero/heroine use strength to achieve his/her goals?

Who are other strong heroes/heroines that you have read about?

How does the hero/heroine show how smart he/she is?

How does the hero's/heroine's intelligence help him/her achieve his/her goals?

Plot

What is the quest or journey that takes place in the story?

How is this journey similar to others that you have read about?

How does the length of the text impact the plot or characters in the story?

What are some of the important events that lead to the climax and resolution?

What challenges does the hero/heroine face?

How does the hero/heroine overcome those challenges?

Is the ending satisfying?

Do epics, legends, and ballads always end happily?

How is the ending different from fairy tale endings you have read?

What would you change about the ending?

Setting

How does the setting of the story influence the characters or events?

Does the setting change to reflect the hero's/heroine's quest or journey?

What challenges faced by the hero/heroine are related to the setting?

Theme

What is (are) the author's message(s)?

How does the quest or journey in the story relate to the theme or message of the story?

What struggle between good and evil is represented in the story?

How does the writer distinguish the good side from the evil side?

Can you relate to the message of the story?

Is the message of the story still valid today?

Style and Language

Why does the story need to be long or include more than one story?

How would the story be different if it were told in prose rather than poetic verse?

How can you tell when the writer is exaggerating?

What figurative language or imagery does the author use to bring the story to life?

What symbolism is there in the story?

What is the mood or tone of the story? Does the mood change?

Myths

MYTHS are stories that seek to explain the beginnings of the world, nature, natural phenomena, or human behavior.

Characteristics of the Genre

What type of traditional literature is this?

What parts of the story help you identify it as a myth?

What characteristics does this myth share with other myths you have read?

What other versions of this myth have you read?

How is this version different from other versions you have read?

Characters

How do the gods act like humans?

What human traits do the gods possess?

How are heroes/heroines represented?

Do heroes/heroines ever defeat gods?

How do heroes/heroines use their wits to defeat gods?

Plot

Which natural phenomena are explained through acts of gods and/or symbolism?

How does this explanation compare to that of the same natural phenomenon from another culture?

How is the struggle between good and evil played out (between characters, within characters)?

What elements of nature are represented or explained in this myth?

How is the problem or question in the myth resolved?

Setting

What is the setting?

What role does nature play in the myth?

How is nature represented?

How is nature represented as good or evil?

Theme

What is (are) the message(s) or lesson(s) in this myth?

Does this myth seek to explain a natural phenomenon?

How do the myths of a civilization represent or guide its religious beliefs or rites?

What is the creation story of this culture and how is it influenced by the environment of the culture?

How does this myth compare to one with a similar theme from another culture?

What influences the differences in myths from different cultures?

Style and Language

How is human behavior revealed symbolically?

Which natural phenomena are explained through acts of gods and/or symbolism?

Modern Fantasy

MODERN FANTASY does not come from an oral tradition, unlike traditional literature. But like traditional literature, modern fantasy stories describe events, places, and people that could not exist in the real world. Modern fantasy texts can be divided into four more specific genres: animal fantasy, low fantasy, high fantasy, and science fiction.

Characteristics of the Genre

What is the genre? How do you know?

How is this book like other books that you have read in this genre?

How is fantasy different from realistic or traditional literature texts?

What are some of the challenges of reading books in this genre?

What are some of the important details or characteristics that make this fantasy?

Is this a good (poor) example of modern fantasy?

What kind of fantasy is this (human characters in fantastic situations; fantasy characters; magical characters)?

What kind of story is this (personified animals, toys, or other inanimate objects; humorous or eccentric characters; preposterous situations; extraordinary worlds; magic or supernatural powers; time shift)?

Which characteristics of fantasy (recurring themes and motifs) did you notice in the text?

Which motifs of fantasy (quest, hero, struggle between good and evil) did you notice in the text?

How does this story compare to another fantasy story with the same topic or theme?

How does this story compare to a story from a different genre in terms of their approaches to similar themes and topics?

How does this story compare to a modern work of fiction that draws on the same themes, patterns of events, or types of characters?

Characters

Who are the characters? Are they portrayed realistically even though they may not be real?

What kinds of characters does the author use (talking animals, magical creatures or people, etc.)? How does this make the story more interesting?

How does the author make the characters seem believable?

How does the author make nonhuman characters (or human characters with magical powers) seem like real people?

How does the culture that the author has created influence the portrayal of characters?

How does the author portray the characters (good, evil, a combination)?

Do the characters make good (bad) choices?

How does the author reveal the characters?

How do characters transform themselves?

What motivates the characters' actions and decisions?

Who is the hero/heroine in the story and what attributes does he/she possess?

Why do you think the author chose to use animals as the main characters?

What human characteristics do the animal characters have?

Do the animal characters remind you of any human characters from other stories?

How does the author make the animal characters seem human?

What special powers do the characters have?

Would you choose to have those powers? Which and why?

How would you use the magic or special powers in the story differently from a character in the story?

What connections do you share with any of the characters?

Which characters remind you of someone in your life?

What choices would you have made if you were the character?

Characters *(continued)*

Do you agree or disagree with a character's choices?

How did you feel about the main character? What did the author do to make you feel that way?

What characters seemed the most real to you? What made you feel that way?

Plot

How do the events and circumstances in this story compare to realistic or historic ones?

What is the problem in the story? Is it unique to fantasy?

How is the problem in the story tied to the events?

What is one step (realistic or fantastic) that the characters took to solve the problem?

How does your knowledge of similar fantasies help you to predict how the events will unfold?

What event from the text can you describe using specific details?

How would you change some of the events in the story, and/or the ending?

How could the problem have been resolved without the use of magic or special powers?

How is the problem often found in fantasy?

Do the events that occur in the story and their outcomes seem logical?

Does the plot seem original or too predictable?

When did you know that the story was a fantasy?

Can you predict how the story will end based on the characters' attributes and decisions?

Can you predict how the story will end based on what you know about the fantasy genre?

What information and details does the author provide to make the story seem realistic even though it couldn't happen?

Plot *(continued)*

How does the plot of this story compare to that in another fantasy story or movie?

What events in the story can you connect to events in your own life?

What challenges do the characters face that are different from the ones that you face?

What events or issues you reminded of anything in your own life?

How did the story make you feel?

How are the problems similar to those in other fantasies you have read?

How does your imagination help you to understand and enjoy fantasy?

What background knowledge helped you to understand this fantasy?

What parts of the story were unfamiliar to you?

Setting

Where and when does this story take place?

How do the setting and time period impact the plot and characters?

Why do you think the author chose this setting and how does that relate to his/her message?

How would the story change if it were set in a different time or place?

What did the author do to create a believable fantasy place?

How does the setting make the story more of a fantasy?

How does this setting compare to settings in other fantasy stories?

What are some of the specific details the author uses to create an authentic fantasy setting?

What details does the author use to show the passage of time?

Was the passage of time realistic or not credible?

How does the setting relate to the plot of the story?

How is the setting similar to a place you know?

Setting *(continued)*

How much time passes in the story?

How does the author help you to enter this imaginary world?

Is the setting symbolic in any way? (Does it represent good, evil, home, or alienation?)

How do different settings from the story compare to each other?

Theme

What does this story make you think about?

What is (are) the author's message(s)?

What universal truths does the author communicate through fantasy?

What recurring themes do you find in this novel and other fantasy novels (quests, magical characters, talking beasts, tricksters)?

What is the author trying to say about society?

How did the author use humor to communicate the message?

How does the author use symbolism to communicate the theme of the story?

How do you think the author's message applies to your life?

What new ideas or perspectives have you gained by reading this text?

What new information about a group have you learned?

How does the structure of the text help to convey meaning or support the genre of fantasy?

How can the lesson or moral of the story be applied to your life?

What understandings about people and life did you derive from the story even though the settings are imaginary?

How do issues in the story relate to issues that occur today?

How is the lesson or moral worthwhile?

How would you summarize the message, lesson, or moral of the story?

Perspective

From whose perspective is the story told?

Why is this the best character to tell the story? Or the best person to be the main character?

How are the perspectives of other characters in conflict with the narrator's perspective?

What perspectives do you agree or disagree with?

What is the author's perspective?

How are perspectives of different groups accurately represented?

Whose point of view is used in the story?

How does the narrator's perspective influence how events are described?

How does the point of view of an imaginary (nonhuman) character influence or change the perspective of a human character?

How do perspectives of characters from different worlds change or influence each other?

Style and Language

How does the author use language to create a fantastical world?

What are some examples of language the author uses to give the story a fantastical feel?

How does the author's style contribute to the genre?

How do the words or style of speaking help to determine the setting?

How does the author use dialogue to give the story the feel of a fantasy?

What words or phrases did the author use to make the story sound like a fantasy?

Why did the author use words or expressions from another language?

Why do you think the author created new words or a new language?

What repetitions or patterns of language did you find in the story?

What are some words or phrases from the story that typically appear in fantasy?

Style and Language *(continued)*

What language does the author use to show that the story took place a long time ago or in the present or future?

How does the author use language to make the story humorous?

What are some examples of words that are magical or powerful?

Figurative Language

Does the author use simile or metaphor to communicate meaning?

What are some examples of simile or metaphor that the author uses?

How does the author use figurative language to help you understand what the imaginary world was like?

Imagery

What imagery does the author use that is typically found in fantasy stories?

How does the language in the story help you to immerse yourself in the setting?

Symbolism

What symbols does the author use to convey meaning? Are the symbols specific to fantasy?

How does the author's use of symbolism help you to better understand the story?

How does the author use symbolism to communicate the theme of the story?

Mood/Tone

What is the mood or tone of this story?

What language does the author use to help establish the mood of the story?

What other elements help to establish the mood of the story?

In what ways does the mood or tone of the story change?

Illustrations/Art

What clues to the setting or meaning do you get through illustrations or other features?

What details does the illustrator include to make the story seem fantastic or unreal?

How do the illustrations help to make the characters and setting come alive?

How does the illustrator's style contribute to the fantasy feel of the book?

What connections do the illustrations have to your own life?

How do the illustrations add symbolic meaning?

Does the mood or tone of the illustrations match the text?

How do the illustrations help/hurt your understanding of the setting, events, or characters?

Design

What do you notice about the design of the book?

Does the book have special features, such as border designs?

How does the design of the book affect your opinion of the book as a whole?

Does the design of the book reflect the genre?

How does the design of the book compare to the design of realistic or traditional literature books you have read?

How does the design of the book compare to the design of other fantasy books you have read?

Believability

Do the characters behave in a way that is expected for the genre?

Do the events and artifacts in the story fit the genre?

Does the dialogue between characters seem authentic to the genre?

Are the characters' emotions and actions presented in a way that is believable given what you know about them?

Quality

Is the plot compelling?

Are the characters well developed?

Is the author's writing style and use of language effective?

Do the illustrations support and enhance the story?

Is the story believable?

Do all of the elements work together?

Animal Fantasy

ANIMAL FANTASY features animal characters who talk and often behave like people.

Characteristics of the Genre

How do you know this is a simple animal fantasy?

In what ways is this story similar to other animal fantasy stories you have read?

How are the numbers 3 or 7 used in the story?

In what other stories have you seen the use of the numbers 3 or 7? How do those stories compare to this one?

What is the significance of the use of the number 3 or 7?

What makes this story easy to understand?

Characters

Do the animal characters talk like humans?

Do the animal characters talk or have human characteristics?

Do characters develop or change in the story?

Plot

How does the story begin?

What is the problem in the story?

What events take place in the story?

How does the story end?

How is the problem resolved?

What makes the ending satisfying or unsatisfying?

Setting

What is the setting?

Does the story take place in the past, present, or future?

How does the time period influence events in the story?

Does the story explain any natural phenomena?

Theme

What is (are) the author's message(s)?

What common themes do you notice?

What lessons do the characters learn?

What did you learn about the culture from which the tale came?

Low Fantasy

LOW FANTASY stories take place in the real world but involve unreal elements such as magic. These stories feature talking animals, toys, and dolls, and characters who have magical powers or use magical objects.

Characteristics of the Genre

How do you know this is low fantasy?

In what ways is this story similar to other low fantasy stories you have read?

How is the language in the story similar to the language in folk and fairy tales?

How has the author made the story believable even though it is not realistic?

Characters

Which characters are able to talk? Would these characters be able to talk in the real world?

What magical powers do characters have?

How do the characters use their magical powers?

How would you use these magical powers?

Are there good characters and evil characters?

Are there any mythical beings that appear in the story?

How do the mythical beings in this story compare to other mythical beings you have read about?

How do the mythical beings compare to what you may already know about them?

What are some of the unusual non-human characters in the story and what do they do?

Who are some of the unusual human characters in the story? What makes them unusual (tiny, large, very strong, etc.)?

Plot

How do the magical powers of the characters affect the plot?

Does the story include magical objects?

How do characters use magical objects?

What does the character need to know in order to use the magical object?

Is there a conflict between good and evil in this story?

How is the conflict between good and evil presented?

Does good triumph over evil in the end?

What makes the ending satisfying or unsatisfying?

Setting

What is the setting?

Does the story take place in medieval times?

Does the story take place in the past, present, or future?

How does the time period influence events in the story?

Does the story take place in another world that does not really exist? How do you know?

What evidence do you have that the story takes place in another world?

How much time passes in the story?

Theme

What is (are) the author's message(s)?

What are the story's big ideas?

How does the genre help to convey the big ideas of the story?

What lessons can you learn for today's world?

How does (do) the message(s) of the story apply to your own life?

High Fantasy

HIGH FANTASY stories feature characters and events that could not exist in the real world. Characters have magical powers or use magical objects, and the setting is either a complete imaginary world, or an alternate imaginary world that exists alongside the real world.

Characteristics of the Genre

How do you know this is high fantasy?

In what ways is this story similar to other high fantasy stories you have read?

How does this book compare to others in the series?

What are some examples of symbolism in the book?

How is the language different from other types of fantasy or traditional literature?

What elements of fantasy did you find in this book (magic, magical objects, heroes, hero's quest, talking animals, etc.)?

Characters

How do the characters grow and change?

How have the characters changed by the end of the story?

How has the author made the characters seem real even though they are not?

How is it possible for ordinary characters to become heroes?

Tell why you think it is realistic that an ordinary character could become a hero.

How would you describe the magical animals in this story?

How do the animals help the characters?

Which characters have mysterious or magical powers?

What are some of the magical or mysterious powers that characters have?

What makes the character's powers mysterious?

How do the characters use their powers?

How do the characters use their powers to defeat or create evil?

How do characters use their powers to complete their missions?

Characters *(continued)*

How does the character succeed in his/her quest?

What keeps the characters from completing their mission or quest?

What is the character searching for?

Who is the wise character who advises the hero?

How does the wise character in this story compare to others in other stories you have read?

How does the wise person remind you of someone in your life?

Plot

How would you describe the conflict between good and evil in the story?

What is the main character's mission or quest?

Does the main character use special powers to complete his/her mission?

Is the ending satisfying or unsatisfying?

How would you change the ending?

Setting

How would you describe the imaginary world where the story takes place?

How do you know the story takes place in two worlds? Is either one our world?

What details does the author use to bring the setting to life?

How much time passes in the story?

Theme

What is (are) the author's message(s)?

What message(s) about human life does the story have?

How does the message of the story apply to your own life?

What is (are) the story's big idea(s)?

How does the genre help to convey the big idea(s) of the story?

What lesson can you learn for today's world?

Science Fiction

SCIENCE FICTION stories feature characters and events that could not exist in the real world. They are characterized by the role that technology or scientific advances play in the narrative, and by futuristic settings.

Characteristics of the Genre

What is the genre? How do you know?

How is this book like other science fiction books?

What are some of the challenges of reading science fiction books?

What are some of the important details that make this science fiction?

What characteristics in the story made you classify it as science fiction?

Is this story a good or poor example of science fiction?

How does this story compare to another science fiction novel on the same topic or theme?

How does this story compare to a story from a different genre in terms of their approaches to similar themes and topics?

How does this story compare to a realistic work of fiction that draws on the same themes, patterns of events, or types of characters?

How does this story compare to a fantasy story?

Could this story really happen? Why or why not?

What scientific or technological content make the text science fiction?

How are science fiction and fantasy similar/different?

Characters

Who are the characters?

Are they portrayed realistically even though they would not be real in our world?

How does the culture that the author has created influence the portrayal of characters?

How does the author portray the characters (good, evil, a combination)?

Characters *(continued)*

Do the characters make good choices? Bad choices? How do you know?

How does the author reveal the characters?

What motivates the characters' actions and decisions?

What choices would you have made if you were the character?

Why do you agree or disagree with a character's choices?

What connections do you share with any of the characters?

What kind of characters has the author used (talking animals, magical creatures or people, etc.)?

How does this makes the story more interesting?

How does the author make these characters seem believable?

What special powers do the characters have?

Why would you choose to have those powers?

How would you use the special powers in the story differently from a character in the story?

Which characters do you feel strongly about? Why?

What does the author do to make you feel that way?

Who is the hero/heroine in the story and what attributes does he/she possess?

How does an imaginary character in this story compare to a human character from another novel?

How does the author make the characters seem human?

How are characters' choices influenced by the unreal world they inhabit?

How are characters' choices similar to the choices that we make in our own world?

Plot

How is the problem in the story tied to events?

How does this story compare with a similar story or movie from another fantasy?

What events in the story connect to events in your own life?

What new information about a real or imaginary group have you learned?

How does your knowledge of similar stories or other science fiction texts help you to predict how the events will unfold?

What challenges do the characters face that are different than the ones that you face?

How would you describe an important event from the story, using specific details?

How does the structure of the text help to convey meaning or support the science fiction genre?

How could the problem in the story have been resolved without the use of special powers or advanced technology (beyond today's capabilities)?

What kinds of problems do you often find in science fiction?

How would you summarize the story, including the message, lesson, or moral and how it is conveyed through key details in the text?

What technology has the author created and how does it relate to the plot?

What are some plausible alternative events and endings for this story?

Based on the characters' attributes and decisions, how do you think the story will end?

What information and details does the author provide to make the story seem realistic even though it couldn't happen?

Based on your own experience and/or knowledge of science fiction, what do you predict will happen to the characters after the story ends?

Setting

Where does the story take place? How is that important to the plot, theme, and characters?

What is the time period? How is that important to the plot, theme, and characters?

How would the story change if it were in a different time or place?

How does the author create a realistic and authentic futuristic world?

Why do you think the author chose this particular setting to tell this story?

Is the setting described believably?

How is the setting like and not like a real place?

How does the author use science and technology to create an imaginary world?

Which scientific or technological ideas or inventions are real and which are imaginary?

How does the setting help to characterize this as a science fiction story?

How does this setting compare to settings in other science fiction stories?

What details in the setting are realistic?

What details did the author use to make the setting seem plausible?

Theme

What is (are) the author's message(s)?

What are some of the recurring themes in other science fiction stories you have read?

How do the events and circumstances in this story compare to realistic or historic ones?

What new ideas or perspectives have you gained by reading this text?

What is the author trying to say about society?

What universal truths does the author communicate through science fiction?

How does the author use symbolism to communicate the theme of the story?

Theme *(continued)*

How can the lesson or moral of the story be applied to your own life?

How do the issues in the story relate to issues that occur today?

What understandings about people and life did you derive from the story even though the settings are science fiction?

Is the lesson or moral of the story worthwhile? Why?

Perspective

From whose perspective is the story told?

Why is this the best character to tell the story or the best person to be the main character?

How are the perspectives of other characters in conflict with the narrator's perspective?

What perspectives do you agree or disagree with?

What is the author's perspective?

How are perspectives of different groups accurately represented?

Does the author seem biased against a particular group even though the group doesn't really exist?

How are characters' perspectives influenced or changed by characters from other worlds?

How does the perspective change when told from a human or non-human narrator?

Does the kind of narrator (human or imaginary) influence your feelings towards the story?

How does the choice of narrator influence the theme?

Style and Language

What are some examples of the language the author uses to give the story a scientific feel?

How does the author's style contribute to the story's genre?

How do the words or style of speaking help to determine the setting?

How does the author use dialogue to give the story a scientific feel?

What words or phrases did the author use to make the story sound futuristic?

Why did the author use words or expressions from another language?

What repetitions or patterns of language did you find in the story?

What are some words or phrases from the story that typically appear in science fiction?

What language does the author use to show that the story took place in the future?

How does the author use language to show a change in setting?

What technological concepts or language were new or difficult for you to comprehend?

How does the author use the technological language of today to create the technology in the text?

Figurative Language

How does the author use figurative language to help you understand imaginary or scientific ideas?

How does the author use simile or metaphor to communicate meaning?

What are some examples of simile or metaphor that the author uses?

How does the author use figurative language to help you understand what the imaginary or futuristic world was like?

Imagery

What imagery does the author use that is typically found in science fiction stories?

How does the language in the story help you to immerse yourself in the setting?

Symbolism

What symbols does the author use to convey meaning? Are the symbols specific to science fiction?

How does the author's use of symbolism help you to better understand the story?

How does the author use symbolism to communicate the theme of the story?

Mood/Tone

What is the mood or tone of this story?

What language does the author use to help establish the mood of the story?

Illustrations/Art

What clues to the setting or meaning do you get from the illustrations or other features of design?

What details does the illustrator include to make the story seem like science fiction?

How does the illustrator use illustrations to make the characters come alive?

How does the illustrator's style contribute to the scientific or futuristic feel of the book?

What connections do the illustrations have to your own life?

How do illustrations add symbolic meaning?

How do the illustrations help you to understand the scientific or technological concepts of the story?

Do the illustrations add to or take away from your pleasure in the story?

Design

What do you notice about the design of the book?

Does the book have special features, such as border designs?

How does the design of the book affect your opinion of the book as a whole?

Does the design of the book reflect the genre?

How does the design of the book compare to the design of realistic or traditional literature books you have read?

How does the design of the book compare to the design of other fantasy or science fiction books you have read?

Believability

Do the characters behave in a way that is expected for the science fiction genre?

Do the events and artifacts in the story fit the science fiction genre?

Does the dialogue between characters seem authentic to the genre?

Are the characters' emotions and actions presented in a way that is believable given what you know about them?

Quality

Is the plot compelling?

Are the characters well developed?

Is the author's writing style and use of language effective?

Do the illustrations support and enhance the story?

Is the story believable?

Do all of the elements work together?

Prompts for Special Types of Fiction Texts

Mystery/Crime Stories

What is the problem in the story? Does it relate to a crime?

What clues to solving the mystery does the author provide?

What do the clues tell you?

Who is seeking to solve the mystery?

The clue _____ led me to realize that _____.

How does the author create suspense?

I predict that _____.

Were your predictions correct?

Was the mystery challenging to solve?

Survival/Adventure Stories

How does the plot of this book differ from other fiction books you've read?

The main character is _____.

I admire this character because _____.

What attributes does the main character rely on to overcome challenges?

How do the characters change?

What is the main character's purpose (quest)?

What events make survival a problem for the character?

How does the setting affect the story?

How does the author create suspense?

What predictions can you make about the character's chances for survival?

Were your predictions correct?

Horror Stories

What elements of fantasy are in the story?

Which characters are victims?

What struggles between good and evil do you see?

Are there good and evil characters?

Are the characters fully realized or are they flat?

Is the story believable or does the writer make animals seem too much like people?

Humorous Stories

What funny comparisons does the author make?

One humorous thing the author said was _____?

What humor did you find in the story?

In what ways was the main character funny?

How did the setting contribute to the humor in this story?

How did the writer create humor?

Short Stories

How is a short story like a novel?

How is a short story different from a novel?

How do the characters change?

Why are the characters, setting, and problem introduced at the beginning of the story?

Where in the story is the problem resolved?

How does the author show the relationships between the characters?

Why do you think the author chose to write a short story instead of a novel?

If this is a collection of short stories, how are the stories related?

What is the overall meaning of the collection?

Animal Stories

Do the animals in the story behave like real animals? Give an example.

What are the relationships between the people and animals in the story?

How do the animal and human characters change?

What do you already know about the type of animals in this story?

Based on what I know about this animal, I think _____ will happen.

Are the animal characters believable?

What is (are) the author's message(s)?

Sports Stories

What can you learn about the main character(s) through the sport?

How does the author build suspense during the games?

How does winning and losing affect the story (the characters)?

How does the main character feel about the sport?

How does the author show the main character's feelings?

What is (are) the author's message (s)?

What does the author say about teamwork?

Series Books

Is this series related to the characters, setting, or theme?

Do the books need to be read in a particular order or do they stand alone?

How are the books related to each other?

What appeals to you about this series?

How would you compare the books in the series to each other?

How do the characters change from one book to another?

What techniques does the author use to get you to want to read the next story in the sequence?

What patterns do you notice in each of the books?

Series Books *(continued)*

What do you think will happen in the next book?

How does the author use illustrations to make the books more interesting or entertaining?

Is the use of illustrations consistent throughout the series?

Picture Books

What are the different features in the book (fonts, sidebars, graphics)?

What do you notice about the illustrations/art?

What did you learn from the peritext?

What did you learn from the illustrations?

How do the illustrations contribute to the mood of the book?

How is the meaning of the story enhanced by the illustrations?

Why would you classify the illustrations as "works of art"?

How is the whole text a "work of art?

How do the art and text fit together?

Which is more essential to understanding the book, the art or the text?

How are picture books similar to/different from short stories?

ABC Books

What is the genre of the book?

How is the information organized?

How is the organization helpful to the reader?

How does the ABC organization complement the text?

How does the organization make the book more interesting or fun to read?

What did you learn from the book?

Why do you think the author chose to present the information or tell the story using the alphabet?

Tell why you would or would not choose to read a book organized by the alphabet.

Prompts for Special Forms of Fiction Texts

Hybrid Texts

What are the genres used in this text?

How do you know what the genres are?

What characteristics help you figure out the genres?

Why is this the best way to give information (tell the story)?

What are some of the challenges of reading books with more than one genre?

How would the story be different if the author used a different genre?

How would the story be different if the author used only one genre?

Graphic Texts (Graphica)

Comic Strip

What is the genre of the comic strip?

What humor did you find in the story?

Does the author/illustrator mock today's society or government? How?

How would you describe the format of the comic strip?

How would you summarize the story?

How do you know that the story will continue in another comic strip?

Does the comic strip stand on its own?

Comic Book

What is the genre of the comic book?

How is the comic book similar to/different from a comic strip?

What impact does the length have on the story?

How would you describe the format of the comic book?

Comic Books *(continued)*

How is the story line carried over from one issue to another?

What are the characters like?

What patterns do you notice in the plots of different comic books?

What common traits do the superheroes have?

How do the superheroes act like humans?

How is the format similar to the format of a magazine?

Graphic Novels

What did you notice about reading this (story, book) in graphic form?

How was reading this graphic text different from reading text only?

How do the pictures in this graphic text help/hinder you as a reader?

What are the challenges of reading graphic texts?

What do you notice about the pictures in the graphic text?

How is the graphic novel similar to/different from a comic book?

How are panels like paragraphs?

How is dialogue displayed?

Why is the dialogue in first person?

How are text boxes used?

What kind of narrator is used in the text boxes?

Which print features help to create mood?

How do print features help the reader to read the text aloud?

In what order should the text be read? How do you know?

How would the novel change if you eliminated the text or the artwork?

Is the artwork as important as the text? Why?

How do the text and artwork work together to create a whole?

Graphic Novel (continued)

How is the gutter used?

What characteristics do graphic novels share with non-graphic novels?

What types of story lines do you find in graphic novels?

If this is an anthology of previously printed comic books, what is the theme that connects the stories?

How do the illustrations help you to predict and confirm outcomes?

How do the illustrations help you to infer the setting, character traits and feelings, and plot?

How do the illustrations help the reader to infer the themes and ideas in the novel?

What aspects of the writer/illustrator's style do you notice?

How would you evaluate the quality of the text and illustrations?

What details in the illustrations convey action?

What details in the illustrations provide insight into a character's feelings or motives?

Manga

How is Manga different from other graphic texts?

How does Manga reflect the Japanese culture?

Why do you think that Manga is separated into stories for girls and stories for boys? How do you feel about that?

How are Manga illustrations different from the illustrations in other graphic novels?

How are the story lines in Manga similar to/different from the story lines in other graphic novels?

What age groups should read Manga? Why?

Electronic Books

How are electronic books similar to paper books?

How are electronic books different from paper books?

What features do you miss when reading an electronic book?

What advantages/disadvantages are there when reading an electronic book?

What options (note-taking, bookmarking, saving citations) have you used when reading an electronic book?

Digital Texts

In what ways do you use digital texts?

How would you compare digital texts to printed texts?

What challenges do digital texts create for the reader?

What information do you find most helpful for completing your task?

Which links are most helpful?

Which links are not helpful?

What kinds of structures are used in the website?

How is the information presented?

Unusual Formats

What kind of format (flip book, pop-up book, two-way book, oversize or life-size book) is used to present the information or story?

How does the format of the book support the text?

How does the format enhance your learning?

How does the format make the information/story more interesting or fun to read?

How do the illustrations make the book more interesting to read?

Is the format distracting? If so, in what ways does it distract you? What format would you choose for the book?